Guilt-Free Girl

Desserts

About Bonnie Marcus

Bonnie Marcus launched her stylish stationery company, the Bonnie Marcus Collection 'where fashion meets paper®,' in 2002 from her dining room table, while expecting her first child. As a former wedding planner in New York City, Marcus was well known for her event planning expertise and found there was a void in the stationery market in terms of fashion-forward stylish designs. She decided to combine her passion for fashion (having worked for designer Diane Von Furstenberg) with her love of event planning and her collection took the stationery industry by storm! Bonnie's stylish designs are now available in thousands of retail stores worldwide and celebrity fans include Cindy Crawford, Christina Aguilera, Britney Spears, Eva Longoria, Marcia Cross and many others. Marcus has been recognized as a pioneer for women in business and is proud to be an established partner of the Breast Cancer Research Foundation® and Autism Speaks®. For further information about the company please visit www.bonniemarcus.com.

Guilt-Free Girl

Desserts

Delicious figure-friendly recipes!

Bonnie Marcus Collection

This edition published under license by Exclusive Editions Publishing Ltd in 2014

Exclusive Editions Publishing Ltd
Chartist House
15–17 Trim Street
Bath BA1 1HA, UK

Copyright © 2013–2014
Illustrations supplied courtesy of the © Bonnie Marcus Collection

Project managed by Cheryl Warner
New recipes and additional text by Robin Donovan
Photography by Ian Garlick
Internal design by Lisa McCormick

ISBN 978-1-4723-2978-3

Printed in China

Notes for the Reader

This book uses both metric and imperial measurements. Follow the same units of
measurement throughout; do not mix metric and imperial. All spoon measurements are
level: teaspoons are assumed to be 5 ml, and tablespoons are assumed to be 15 ml.
Unless otherwise stated, milk is assumed to be full fat, eggs and individual vegetables
are medium, and pepper is freshly ground black pepper. Unless otherwise stated, all root
vegetables should be peeled prior to using.

Garnishes, decorations and serving suggestions are all optional and not necessarily
included in the recipe ingredients or method. Any optional ingredients and seasoning to
taste are not included in the nutritional analysis. The times given are an approximate guide
only. Preparation times differ according to the techniques used by different people and the
cooking times may also vary from those given. Optional ingredients, variations or serving
suggestions have not been included in the time calculations.

Nutritional values are per serving or per item (for Makes…). Consult your doctor before
following any new diet or fitness plans.

Contents

The Guilt-free Life

What girl doesn't want to eat her cake and look good doing it? Well, now you can with this guilt-free collection of recipes! The desserts in this book let you indulge in delicious sweet treats without any of the usual regrets as these recipes are all low in calories and low in fat. What could be more perfect?

If you thought you had to give up sinfully tasty desserts in order to look and feel healthy, think again. You can (and, as far as we're concerned, should!) enjoy delicious food – even amazing puddings – as part of a healthy lifestyle. The key isn't deprivation at all, but moderation. Pick your moments, watch your portion size, look for nutrient-dense ingredients and choose desserts with the most intense flavours so that you get deep satisfaction from every bite.

From perfect little bites such as our spicy Chai Tea Biscuits made with wholemeal flour, rich Fig & Hazelnut Biscotti or super-light and tangy Lemon Meringue Biscuits, to dinner party showstoppers such as our oozy Mini Chocolate Fondants and architecturally stunning Strawberry & White Chocolate Mousse Napoleons, the desserts you'll find here will satisfy your most intense cravings. Bursting with flavour, they'll never leave you feeling deprived. They are big on flavour, but each is surprisingly low in calories and fat.

We've got sweet treats for casual gatherings, quick snacks to satisfy a sweet tooth in a hurry and elaborate desserts that are sure to be a highlight of any party. And the best thing is that with fewer than 250 calories per serving, each and every one will leave you feeling lithe and lovely and ready to take on the world. Come and join the guilt-free revolution!

The Perfect Little Bite

Chai Tea Biscuits

 calories 55 fat 3.1g sat fat 1.9g total sugars 3.7g carbs 6.5g

INGREDIENTS
makes 30

100 g/3½ oz soft light brown sugar
2 tbsp dry chai tea (about 4 teabags)
¼ tsp salt
125 g/4½ oz wholemeal flour, plus extra for dusting
1 tsp vanilla extract
115 g/4 oz cold, unsalted butter

METHOD

1 Preheat the oven to 180°C/350°F/Gas Mark 4 and line a baking tray with baking paper.

2 Put the brown sugar, tea and salt into a food processor and whizz until the tea has been ground to a fine powder. Add the flour, vanilla extract and butter and process until well combined and the mixture begins to hold together. If the mixture is too dry, add cold water, ½ teaspoon at a time, and whizz until the mixture just comes together. Turn out the dough on to a sheet of clingfilm and shape into a log. Wrap tightly and refrigerate for 15 minutes.

3 Roll out the dough on a lightly floured surface to about 3 mm/⅛ inch thick and cut into rounds, using a round 6-cm/2½-inch biscuit cutter (or use the shape of your choice). Transfer the biscuits to the prepared baking tray and bake in the preheated oven for 18–20 minutes or until they begin to colour.

4 Remove from the oven and transfer the biscuits to a wire rack to cool completely. Serve at room temperature.

Sesame, Marshmallow & Cranberry Squares

calories 124	fat 5.3g	sat fat 0.6g	total sugars 12.3g	carbs 19g

INGREDIENTS
makes 20

150 g/5½ oz porridge oats
50 g/1¾ oz sesame seeds
3 tbsp soft light brown sugar
40 g/1½ oz mini marshmallows
70 g/2½ oz dried cranberries
115 g/4 oz honey
5 tbsp sunflower oil,
    plus extra for greasing
a few drops of vanilla extract

METHOD

1 Preheat the oven to 160°C/325°F/Gas Mark 3. Lightly brush a 28 x 18-cm/11 x 7-inch baking tin with oil. Line the base with non-stick baking paper.

2 Put the oats, sesame seeds, sugar, marshmallows and cranberries into a mixing bowl and stir. Make a well in the centre, add the honey, oil and vanilla extract, then stir again.

3 Press the mixture into the prepared baking tin and level, using a metal spoon. Bake in the preheated oven for 20 minutes or until a golden colour and bubbling.

4 Leave to cool in the tin for 10 minutes, then cut into small squares and leave to cool completely before turning out of the tin. Serve or store in an airtight container in a cool, dry place for up to two days.

Pecan Nut Caramel Bars

 calories 224

 fat 9.3g

 sat fat 3g

 total sugars 23.3g

 carbs 32.6g

INGREDIENTS

makes 12

base

cooking spray
100 g/3½ oz soft light brown
    sugar
55 g/2 oz butter
55 g/2 oz wholemeal flour
55 g/2 oz plain flour
2 tsp water

filling

2 eggs
165 g/5¾ oz soft brown sugar
1 tbsp plain flour
1 tsp vanilla extract
¼ tsp salt
85 g/3 oz pecan nut pieces

METHOD

1 Preheat the oven to 190°C/375°F/Gas Mark 5. Spray a 28 x 18-cm/11 x 7-inch baking tin with cooking spray.

2 To make the base, cream together the brown sugar and butter in a medium-size bowl, using an electric whisk. Add both flours and the water and mix until combined. Transfer the mixture to the prepared baking tin and cover the base of the tin in an even layer. Bake in the preheated oven for about 12–15 minutes until lightly coloured. Remove from the oven, but leave the oven on.

3 While the base is baking, make the filling. Beat the eggs, brown sugar, flour, vanilla extract and salt in a large bowl with an electric whisk until well combined. Stir in the pecan nut pieces and pour the mixture over the warm base in the baking tin. Bake in the preheated oven for 18–20 minutes or until the filling begins to colour around the edges.

4 Remove from the oven and transfer to a wire rack to cool completely.

5 Cut into 12 squares and serve at room temperature.

White & Dark Chocolate-dipped Strawberries

 calories 54
 fat 3g
 sat fat 1.7g
 total sugars 5g
 carbs 6.3g

INGREDIENTS
makes 24

115 g/4 oz plain chocolate, roughly chopped
115 g/4 oz white chocolate, roughly chopped
24 large strawberries

METHOD

1 Line a baking tray with baking paper. Put the plain chocolate and white chocolate into two separate heatproof bowls, set the bowls over two saucepans of gently simmering water and heat until melted.

2 Dip the pointed end of each strawberry into one of the melted chocolates and transfer it to the prepared baking tray. Leave to cool for 1 hour, or until set.

3 Put each strawberry in a liqueur glass or on a plate and serve immediately.

Toffee Popcorn Bites

 calories 230
 fat 7.5g
 sat fat 2.5g
 total sugars 38g
 carbs 44g

INGREDIENTS
serves 8
100 g/3½ oz caster sugar
100 g/3½ oz soft light
brown sugar
125 ml/4 fl oz golden syrup
25 g/1 oz butter
1½ tsp bicarbonate of soda
1 tsp salt
½ tsp vanilla extract
60 g/2¼ oz plain, air-popped
popcorn

METHOD

1 Cover a large baking tray with baking paper or foil.

2 In a saucepan, combine the sugars, golden syrup and butter and bring to the boil over a medium–high heat. Reduce the heat to medium and boil, without stirring, for 4 minutes. Carefully stir in the bicarbonate of soda, salt and vanilla extract.

3 Put the popcorn in a large mixing bowl. Pour the toffee over the popcorn and stir to coat. Using two spoons, form the mixture into 24 balls, about 6 cm/2½ inches in diameter, and place them on the lined baking tray. Leave to sit at room temperature for about 1 hour or until firm. Serve at room temperature.

Crispy Chocolate, Fruit & Nut Bark

calories 153 | fat 9.6g | sat fat 4.8g | total sugars 10.4g | carbs 15.5g

INGREDIENTS
makes 16

70 g/2½ oz dried cherries
55 g/2 oz hazelnuts, chopped
350 g/12 oz plain chocolate, chopped
15 g/½ oz crispy rice cereal

METHOD

1 Line a 28 x 23-cm/11 x 9-inch baking tin with baking paper.

2 Combine the cherries and hazelnuts in a small bowl and mix well.

3 Put the chocolate in a heatproof bowl set over a saucepan of gently simmering water and heat, stirring frequently, until the chocolate has melted. Remove from the heat and stir in the rice cereal.

4 Pour the chocolate mixture into the prepared tin and smooth it into a thin layer, using a rubber palette knife. Immediately top with the cherries and nuts, sprinkling them evenly over the top. Press the cherries and nuts into the chocolate with the palm of your hand. Refrigerate for at least 1 hour until completely set.

5 Break into pieces and serve at room temperature.

Lemon Meringue Biscuits

calories 73 | fat 0g | sat fat 0g | total sugars 17g | carbs 18g

INGREDIENTS
serves 8

2 egg whites
⅛ tsp cream of tartar
pinch of salt
140 g/5 oz caster sugar
finely grated zest of 1 lemon

METHOD

1 Preheat the oven to 110°C/225°F/Gas Mark ¼. Line a large baking tray with foil or baking paper.

2 Beat the egg whites with an electric whisk on high speed in a medium-size bowl until they are frothy. Add the cream of tartar and salt and continue to beat on high until soft peaks form. Gradually add the sugar and continue to beat on high for about 3–4 minutes or until stiff peaks form. Fold in the lemon zest.

3 Drop the mixture in rounded teaspoons on to the prepared baking tray. Bake in the preheated oven for about 1½ hours or until dry and crisp but not yet beginning to colour. Turn off the oven and leave the biscuits to sit inside for a further 30 minutes. Serve at room temperature.

Mocha-filled Filo Cases

calories 183 | fat 6.5g | sat fat 3.5g | total sugars 19g | carbs 27g

INGREDIENTS
makes 8
filo cases
3 sheets frozen filo pastry, thawed
cooking spray
1 tsp caster sugar
halved strawberries, to serve (optional)

filling
115 g/4 oz plain chocolate, chopped
3 tbsp cocoa powder
about 200 ml/7 fl oz water
1 tsp vanilla extract
1 tbsp instant espresso powder
100 g/3½ oz caster sugar
3 egg whites
¼ tsp cream of tartar

METHOD
1 Preheat the oven to 180°C/350°F/Gas Mark 4.

2 To make the filo cases, carefully separate one filo sheet from the others, lay it on a work surface and spritz it all over with the cooking spray. Sprinkle it with about one third of the sugar. Lay a further sheet of filo over the top of the first and repeat the steps until you have three layers, ending with a sprinkling of sugar. Cut the stack of filo sheets into eight rectangles, and place each rectangle into an ungreased hole in a muffin tin, pressing down to form a case out of the filo. Bake the filo cases in the preheated oven for about 6–8 minutes or until lightly coloured. Remove from the oven and leave to cool in the tin for several minutes, then transfer to a wire rack to cool completely before removing from the tin.

3 To make the filling, put the chocolate, cocoa and 5 tablespoons of water in a heatproof bowl set over a saucepan of gently simmering water, and heat, stirring frequently, until the chocolate has completely melted and the mixture is smooth. Remove from the heat and stir in the vanilla extract and espresso powder. Remove the bowl from the saucepan and set aside.

4 In a small saucepan, combine the sugar with 125 ml/4 fl oz water and bring to the boil. Cook, stirring, for about 5 minutes or until the mixture begins to thicken.

5 Beat the egg whites in large bowl with an electric whisk until foamy. Add the cream of tartar and beat, gradually increasing the speed, until soft peaks form. With the whisk running, slowly add the warm sugar mixture. Increase the speed to high and beat until the mixture has cooled and stiff, glossy peaks form.

6 Whisk one third of the egg white mixture into the chocolate mixture until it is well combined. Whisk in the remaining egg white mixture. Transfer to a medium-size bowl and cover with clingfilm, pressing it directly on to the surface to prevent a skin forming. Chill in the refrigerator for at least 1 hour.

7 Just before serving, scoop the filling into a piping bag fitted with a large star nozzle. Pipe the filling into the filo cases, dividing it equally between them. Serve immediately, with halved strawberries if liked.

Live Life to the Full!

Live your life the guilt-free way! Eating should be enjoyable, so why cram yourself into a harsh dieting lifestyle that makes you miserable? You absolutely can enjoy an active lifestyle and be as healthy as you've always dreamt of being while eating delicious food – even deeply satisfying desserts such as the ones on these pages. These recipes are low in calories and fat, so there is no guilt!

The key to enjoying life to its fullest – including eating delicious, satisfying food – while staying healthy is moderation. If you swear off whole categories of foods, you run the risk of creating an obsession so intense that you'll spend your days thinking about nothing but buttercream icing and chocolate cake. If, on the other hand, you call a truce with those 'forbidden' foods and allow all things in moderation, you'll be able to satisfy those urges and move on, perhaps even have time and energy for a brisk walk or an invigorating workout at the gym. The guilt-free way is simple!

Make wise choices and you'll be on the right path. Our Maple & Nut Flapjacks make for a wonderful, protein- and fibre-packed treat. Eat just one and you get a ton of nutrition, not to mention enjoyment.

If a cheeseburger and chips is what you're craving, make it a turkey burger stuffed with spinach, herbs and feta cheese. Switch the chips for baked sweet potato chips, which are full of vitamins. You'll end up feeling completely satisfied without wasting an entire day's worth of calories on one gut-busting meal.

If chocolate cake is the only thing that will do, try our Mini Chocolate Fondants, which are flourless, relatively low in sugar and full of rich, plain chocolate flavour. If it's cheesecake you want, try our Berry & Rhubarb Cheesecake Bars. They pack all the flavour and creamy, rich cheesecakiness you love in a lightened-up package.

And remember, being a guilt-free girl is all about having the food and flavours you love!

Maple & Nut Flapjacks

 calories 200

 fat 10g

 sat fat 1.5g

 total sugars 11g

 carbs 22.8g

INGREDIENTS
makes 12

cooking spray
140 g/5 oz porridge oats
55 g/2 oz pecan nuts, chopped
55 g/2 oz flaked almonds
125 ml/4 fl oz maple syrup
55 g/2 oz soft light brown sugar
60 g/2¼ oz smooth peanut
   butter
1 tsp vanilla extract
¼ tsp salt
55 g/2 oz puffed rice cereal
30 g/1 oz ground linseeds
   (flaxseeds)

METHOD

1 Preheat the oven to 180°C/350°F/Gas Mark 4. Coat a 33 x 23-cm/13 x 9-inch baking dish with cooking spray.

2 Combine the oats, pecan nuts and almonds in a large baking tin and toast in the preheated oven for 5–7 minutes or until lightly coloured.

3 While the oats and nuts are toasting, combine the maple syrup, brown sugar and peanut butter in a small saucepan and bring to the boil over a medium heat. Cook, stirring, for about 4–5 minutes or until the mixture thickens slightly. Stir in the vanilla extract and salt.

4 When the oats and nuts are toasted, place them in a mixing bowl and add the rice cereal and linseeds. Add the syrup mixture to the oat mixture and stir to combine. Spread the mixture into the prepared baking dish and chill for at least 1 hour before cutting into 12 bars. Serve at room temperature. Store in a tightly covered container.

Fig & Hazelnut Biscotti

 calories 182

 fat 7.3g

 sat fat 2g

 total sugars 14g

 carbs 26g

INGREDIENTS
makes 18

125 g/4½ oz plain flour
125 g/4½ oz wholemeal flour
½ tsp baking powder
½ tsp bicarbonate of soda
¼ tsp salt
55 g/2 oz unsalted butter, softened
100 g/3½ oz caster sugar
55 g/2 oz soft brown sugar
1 tbsp vanilla extract
1 tbsp orange zest
2 eggs
85 g/3 oz hazelnuts, chopped and toasted
200 g/7 oz dried figs, chopped

METHOD

1 Preheat the oven to 180°C/350°F/Gas Mark 4. Line a baking tray with baking paper.

2 Combine the flours, baking powder, bicarbonate of soda and salt in a medium-size bowl.

3 Use an electric whisk to cream together the butter and sugars in a large bowl. Add the vanilla extract and orange zest, then the eggs, one at a time, beating after each addition. Add half of the flour mixture and mix until combined. Add the remaining flour mixture along with the nuts and figs. Mix until incorporated.

4 Turn out the dough on to the prepared baking tray and shape into two loaves, about 20 x 7.5 cm/8 x 3 inches. Bake in the preheated oven for about 30–35 minutes or until a golden colour. Remove from the oven and leave to cool for 10–15 minutes. Reduce the oven heat to 160°C/325°F/Gas Mark 3.

5 Slice the loaves on the diagonal into 2.5 cm/1 inch-thick pieces and place them on end on the baking tray so that both cut sides are exposed. Bake for about 25 minutes or until lightly coloured.

6 Remove from the oven and transfer to a wire rack to cool completely before serving.

Super-chilled!

Frozen Yogurt Cups

calories 26 | fat 0.4g | sat fat 0.2g | total sugars 4g | carbs 4g

INGREDIENTS
makes 12
450 g/1 lb low-fat natural yogurt
1½ tbsp finely grated
   orange rind
250 g/9 oz mixed berries, such
   as blueberries, raspberries
   and strawberries, plus
   extra to decorate
fresh mint sprigs, to decorate
   (optional)

METHOD
1 Set the freezer to its coldest setting at least 2 hours before freezing this dish. Line a 12-hole muffin tin with 12 paper cases, or use small ramekin dishes placed on a baking tray.

2 Mix together the yogurt and orange rind in a large bowl. Cut any large strawberries into pieces so that they are the same size as the blueberries and raspberries.

3 Add the fruit to the yogurt, then spoon into the cases or ramekins. Freeze for 2 hours, or until just frozen. Decorate with extra fruit and mint sprigs, if using, and serve. Return the freezer to its original setting afterwards.

Banana & Coconut Ice Cream Balls

 calories 173   fat 10g   sat fat 5g   total sugars 12.3g   carbs 20g

INGREDIENTS
serves 6

3 ripe bananas
4 tbsp evaporated milk
75 g/2¾ oz plain chocolate, cut into small pieces
1 tbsp rapeseed oil
3 tbsp desiccated coconut

METHOD

1 Peel and cut the bananas into small pieces. Put into a freezerproof container and freeze for at least 2 hours. Transfer the frozen bananas to a food processor or blender and add the evaporated milk. Whizz until smooth and creamy. Scrape the mixture into a freezerproof container, cover and freeze for a further hour or so, until the mixture is firm.

2 Put the chocolate and oil in a heatproof bowl set over a saucepan of gently simmering water, and heat, stirring frequently, until melted. Place the coconut in a bowl.

3 Line a baking tray with baking paper. Use a small scoop (such as a melon baller) to create 5-cm/2-inch balls of the banana mixture and set them on the prepared baking tray. If the balls begin to soften, place them in the freezer for 15 minutes or until they are firm again. Working quickly, spear an ice cream ball with a cocktail stick and dunk it into the melted chocolate, twirling to coat completely. Allow the excess chocolate to drip off, then transfer the ball to the bowl of desiccated coconut and turn to coat lightly.

4 Place the balls on the baking paper and continue until all of the ice cream balls are coated in chocolate. Place the baking tray in the freezer for a few minutes, chill until firm and serve immediately.

Eat the Guilt-free Foods You Love!

A guilt-free girl wants the best of both worlds – delicious flavours and a healthy lifestyle! But eating healthily doesn't have to be an excruciating exercise in deprivation. It's really more about making good choices and smart substitutions. Think of it as a way to feel great, have more energy and be happy, all while keeping your body as healthy as possible. Eating a healthy, guilt-free diet is just a matter of making everything you eat as good for you as possible without adding any empty calories.

Boosting the nutrition of your favourite recipes is really as easy as switching handbags, or, more specifically, substituting whole grains – such as wholemeal or brown rice flour, or even quinoa or amaranth flour – for processed white flour. Our Chai Tea Biscuits and Pecan Nut Caramel Bars are perfect examples of how easy it is to boost nutrition without sacrificing flavour.

Substituting fruits and other natural sweeteners for refined sugar is another way to boost the nutritional content of foods, while also reducing their calories. Apple sauce, puréed ripe pears or bananas, and agave syrup are great ways to sweeten food without a lot of empty calories (or scary chemicals). Our spicy and moist Lemon-glazed Gingerbread Cake, for instance, is sweetened with apple sauce.

Using healthy fats, such as those from avocadoes, olives, nuts and seeds, also makes foods healthier without detracting from their appeal. Our Almond Cupcakes with Poached Pears, for example, get most of their richness from ground almonds, which delivers a type of fat that may help to lower cholesterol and reduce the risk of certain illnesses.

By simply cutting down on saturated fats such as butter and cream, you can give some of your favourite puddings a healthy makeover. Key Lime Pie made with fewer egg yolks (more egg whites), fat-free sweetened condensed milk and fat-free yogurt is far lighter and healthier than the classic variety. Likewise, using egg whites in place of cream in chocolate mousse, as in our Mocha-filled Filo Cases, is ingenious, even if we do say so ourselves.

If you want to be super-extra smart, try adding a few 'super-foods' ingredients, which are densely packed with nutrients, to your favourite recipes. For example, add a few tablespoons of ground linseeds (flaxseeds) to muffins or brownies, dried goji berries to a milkshake or smoothie, or chia seeds for a little extra crunch in your shortbread biscuits.

Mochaccino Pops

 calories 69 fat 0.5g sat fat 0.3g total sugars 12g carbs 13.5g

INGREDIENTS
makes 6

225 ml/8 fl oz cold skimmed milk
1 tsp powdered gelatine
5 tbsp strong brewed coffee
    or espresso
50 g/1¾ oz sugar
25 g/1 oz cocoa powder
½ tsp vanilla extract

METHOD

1 Pour the milk into a medium-size bowl and sprinkle the gelatine over the top. Leave to sit for about 5 minutes or until the gelatine has softened.

2 In a small saucepan, heat the coffee over a medium heat until hot but not boiling. Add the sugar and cocoa powder, remove from the heat and whisk until the sugar and cocoa powder have dissolved. Add the vanilla extract.

3 Slowly whisk the milk mixture into the warm coffee mixture. Continue whisking for about 3 minutes or until the gelatine has completely dissolved. Pour the mixture into six mini ice pop moulds, insert the sticks and freeze for at least 4 hours or overnight. Serve frozen.

Red Wine Sorbet

 calories 166 fat 0g sat fat 0g total sugars 22g carbs 23g

INGREDIENTS
serves 6

1 orange
1 lemon
600 ml/1 pint fruity red wine
140 g/5 oz soft light brown sugar
300 ml/10 fl oz water, chilled
2 egg whites, lightly beaten
fresh fruit, to serve

METHOD

1 Peel the zest from the orange and lemon in strips, using a vegetable peeler, taking care not to remove any of the bitter white pith underneath. Place in a saucepan with the red wine and sugar. Heat gently, stirring until the sugar dissolves, then bring to the boil and simmer for 5 minutes. Remove from the heat and stir in the water.

2 Squeeze the juice from the fruit. Stir into the wine mixture. Cover and leave to sit until completely cool, then sieve into a freezerproof container. Cover and freeze for 7–8 hours, or until firm.

3 Working quickly, break the sorbet into chunks and transfer to a food processor. Blend for a few seconds to break down the chunks, then, leaving the processor running, gradually pour the egg whites through the feed tube. The mixture will become paler. Continue blending until smooth.

4 Freeze for a further 3–4 hours or until firm. Scoop into six chilled glasses or dishes and serve immediately with the fresh fruit.

Lemon Buttermilk Sorbet

calories	fat	sat fat	total sugars	carbs
176	1.6g	1g	37.8g	38.6g

INGREDIENTS
serves 6

1 tbsp finely grated lemon zest
4 tbsp fresh lemon juice
1 tbsp fresh lime juice
200 g/7 oz caster sugar
500 ml/18 fl oz buttermilk

METHOD

1 If you are using an ice-cream maker, freeze the insert of your ice-cream maker for at least 24 hours.

2 In a medium-size bowl, combine the lemon zest, lemon and lime juices and sugar and whisk until the sugar is fully dissolved. Add the buttermilk and whisk to combine. Cover the bowl and chill the mixture in the refrigerator for at least 3–4 hours, or overnight if desired, until it is cold.

3 If you are using an ice-cream maker, transfer the mixture to the frozen insert of your ice-cream maker and churn according to the manufacturer's instructions for about 30–60 minutes, or until firm. Transfer to a freezerproof container, cover and store in the freezer. Alternatively, pour the mixture into a freezerproof container, cover with clingfilm and freeze for about 2 hours or until it has begun to harden around the edges. Beat until smooth to get rid of any ice crystals. Freeze again, repeat the process twice, then freeze until it is completely firm.

4 Serve straight from the freezer.

Fruit Cocktail Pops

calories 56	fat 0.3g	sat fat trace	total sugars 11g	carbs 14g

INGREDIENTS
makes 8
225 g/8 oz strawberries, hulled
2 small ripe peaches, peeled,
    stoned and roughly chopped
    (or 250 g/9 oz canned
    peaches, drained)
4 large kiwi fruits, peeled and
    roughly chopped

sugar syrup
2 tbsp caster sugar
5 tbsp water

METHOD
1 To make the sugar syrup, put the sugar and water into a saucepan over a low heat and stir until the sugar has dissolved. Increase the heat until boiling, then simmer for 3–4 minutes. Remove the pan from the heat and leave the sugar syrup to cool completely before using.

2 Put the strawberries in a blender and whizz until puréed. Stir in 2 tablespoons of the sugar syrup. Pour the mixture into eight 125-ml/4 fl-oz ice pop moulds. Freeze for 2 hours or until firm.

3 When the strawberry mixture is frozen, put the peaches in the blender and whizz until puréed. Stir in half of the remaining sugar syrup. Pour the peach mixture over the frozen strawberry mixture. Insert the ice pop sticks and freeze for 2 hours, or until firm.

4 When the peach mixture is frozen, put the kiwi fruits in the blender and whizz until puréed. Stir in the remaining sugar syrup. Pour the kiwi mixture over the frozen peach mixture and freeze for 2 hours, or until firm.

5 To unmould the ice pops, dip the frozen moulds into warm water for a few seconds and gently release the pops while holding the sticks.

Frozen Hot Chocolate with Hazelnut Liqueur

calories 242 · fat 8.7g · sat fat 4.9g · total sugars 23g · carbs 35g

INGREDIENTS
makes 4

85 g/3 oz plain chocolate, chopped
2 tbsp caster sugar
1 tbsp cocoa powder
350 ml/12 fl oz skimmed milk
900 g/2 lb ice cubes
1 medium banana
4 tbsp hazelnut liqueur

METHOD

1 Put the chocolate into a heatproof bowl set over a saucepan of gently simmering water and heat, stirring frequently, until the chocolate has melted.

2 Add the sugar and cocoa powder and heat, stirring constantly, until the sugar has completely dissolved. Remove from the heat and slowly add the milk, stirring until combined. Leave to cool to room temperature.

3 Transfer the chocolate mixture to a blender and add the ice, banana and hazelnut liqueur. Blend until well combined and frothy. Pour into 4 cups and serve immediately.

Maple Ice Cream with Nut-crunch Topping

 calories 193
 fat 3.2g
 sat fat 0.6g
 total sugars 30g
 carbs 35.7g

INGREDIENTS

serves 6

ice cream

500 ml/18 fl oz skimmed milk

225 ml/8 fl oz light evaporated milk

200 ml/7 fl oz maple syrup

½ tsp maple or vanilla extract

topping

1 tsp unsalted butter

1 tbsp soft light brown sugar

20 g/¾ oz corn flakes cereal, crushed

2 tbsp pecan nut pieces

METHOD

1 If you are using an ice-cream maker, freeze the insert of your ice-cream maker for at least 24 hours.

2 In a medium-size bowl, combine the milks, maple syrup and maple extract and stir to combine well. Cover and chill in the refrigerator for 3 hours (or longer), or until cold.

3 If you are using an ice-cream maker, transfer the mixture to the freezer insert of your ice-cream maker and churn according to the manufacturer's instructions for about 30–60 minutes, or until firm. Transfer to a freezerproof container, cover and store in the freezer. Alternatively, pour the mixture into a freezerproof container, cover with clingfilm and freeze for about 2 hours, or until it has begun to harden around the edges. Beat until smooth to get rid of any ice crystals. Freeze again, repeat the process twice, then freeze until it is completely firm.

4 To make the topping, cover a baking tray with baking paper. Melt the butter in a small saucepan over a medium heat. Add the brown sugar and stir to combine. Remove the pan from the heat and add the cereal flakes and pecan nut pieces, stirring to coat. Transfer the mixture to the prepared baking tray and leave to cool to room temperature.

5 Serve the ice cream straight from the freezer and sprinkle with the nut-crunch topping.

Mini Clementine Sorbets

 calories 73
 fat trace
 sat fat trace
 total sugars 16g
 carbs 19g

INGREDIENTS
makes 10

10 clementines
70 g/2½ oz caster sugar
4 tbsp water
finely grated rind and juice of
    1 lemon
juice of 1 large orange

METHOD

1 Cut a thin slice off the top of each clementine and set aside. Squeeze a little of the juice from each fruit into a blender. Using a teaspoon, scoop the flesh into the blender, then whizz to a purée.

2 Press the purée through a sieve into a large loaf tin. Put the 10 clementine shells into a roasting tin and freeze to make cups.

3 Put the sugar and water into a heavy-based saucepan. Heat gently for 5 minutes or until the sugar has dissolved, tilting the pan to mix them together. Increase the heat and boil rapidly without stirring for 1 minute. Remove from the heat, then stir in the lemon rind and juice. Pour the lemon syrup and orange juice through a sieve and on to the clementine purée, stir, then leave to cool.

4 Transfer the loaf tin to the freezer and freeze for 2 hours, or until the mixture is semi-frozen. Break up the ice crystals using a fork, then return to the freezer for 1 hour. Beat again with the fork, then freeze for a further hour. Beat again until it resembles coloured snow.

5 Spoon the sorbet into the clementine cups, add the lids at a slanted angle and freeze overnight. (If the sorbet has frozen too firmly, leave it to soften at room temperature for a few minutes, then beat with a fork.) When ready to serve, transfer the iced desserts to a plate.

Sorbet Sandwiches

 calories 154
 fat 2.2g
 sat fat 1.1g
 total sugars 25.5g
 carbs 32.6g

INGREDIENTS

makes 8

sorbet

125 g/4½ oz caster sugar
300 ml/10 fl oz water
finely grated rind of 2 limes
175 ml/6 fl oz lime juice
(from about 8 limes)

biscuits

30 g/1 oz plain flour,
plus extra for dusting
30 g/1 oz wholemeal flour
¼ tsp bicarbonate of soda
⅛ tsp salt
¾ tsp ground ginger
¼ tsp ground cinnamon
pinch of ground cloves
15 g/½ oz unsalted butter
2 tbsp caster sugar
2 tbsp dark brown sugar
1 egg
1½ tbsp treacle

METHOD

1 To make the sorbet, combine the sugar and 150 ml/5 fl oz of the water in a small saucepan and bring to the boil. Reduce the heat to a simmer and cook, stirring, for about 2 minutes or until the sugar has fully dissolved. In a medium-size bowl, combine the sugar syrup with the remaining 150 ml/5 fl oz water, and the lime rind and juice. Chill in the refrigerator for about 3 hours (or longer) until cold.

2 Pour the mixture into the chilled insert of an ice-cream machine. Churn and freeze according to the manufacturer's instructions. Alternatively, pour the mixture into a shallow freezerproof container, cover with clingfilm and freeze for about 2 hours until beginning to harden around the edges. Beat until smooth to get rid of any ice crystals. Freeze again, repeat the process twice, then freeze until completely firm.

3 To make the biscuits, preheat the oven to 180°C/350°F/ Gas Mark 4. Line a baking tray with baking paper. In a medium-size bowl, combine the flours, bicarbonate of soda, salt, ginger, cinnamon and cloves. In a large bowl, cream together the butter and the white and brown sugars until light and fluffy. Add the egg and treacle and mix until incorporated. Add the dry ingredients to the butter mixture and beat on medium speed, scraping down the sides of the bowl once or twice, until incorporated. Refrigerate the mixture for about 15 minutes.

4 Lightly dust the work surface with flour and form the biscuit mixture into 16 balls, about 4 cm/1½ inches in diameter. Flatten the balls into rounds about 7.5 cm/ 3 inches across and 5 mm/⅛ inch thick and place them a few inches apart on the prepared baking tray. Bake in the preheated oven for about 12–14 minutes or until the biscuits are beginning to crisp. Remove from the oven and transfer the biscuits to a wire rack to cool completely.

5 To make the sandwiches, place a scoop of the frozen sorbet on to the flat side of a biscuit, then press a further biscuit on top. Scrape off any sorbet that squeezes out the sides into the sorbet container. Repeat until you have eight sandwiches. Wrap the sandwiches individually in baking paper or clingfilm and store in the freezer. Remove from the freezer about 15 minutes before serving.

Chewy Chocolate Cookies

 calories 79
 fat 3.2g
 sat fat 1.9g
 total sugars 7.5g
 carbs 12g

INGREDIENTS
makes 30

150 g/5½ oz plain flour,
    plus extra for dusting
25 g/1 oz cocoa powder
¼ tsp bicarbonate of soda
¼ tsp salt
200 g/7 oz caster sugar
85 g/3 oz unsalted butter,
    softened
3 egg whites
1 tsp vanilla extract
40 g/1½ oz plain chocolate
    chips

METHOD

1 Preheat the oven to 180°C/350°F/Gas Mark 4. Line two baking trays with baking paper.

2 In a medium-size bowl, combine the flour, cocoa powder, bicarbonate of soda and salt.

3 In a large bowl, use an electric whisk to cream together the sugar and butter until fluffy. Add the egg whites, vanilla extract and chocolate chips and mix until well combined.

4 Lightly flour your hands and form rounded tablespoons of the cookie mixture into balls. Put these on to the prepared baking trays, setting them about 5 cm/2 inches apart. Bake in the preheated oven for 10–12 minutes or until set.

5 Transfer the cookies to a wire rack to cool completely before serving.

Raisin Apple Turnovers

 calories 130 fat 1.1g sat fat trace total sugars 11.7g carbs 27.4g

INGREDIENTS
makes 6
cooking spray
1 cooking apple, peeled, cored and diced
2 tbsp raisins
2 tbsp light brown sugar
6 sheets frozen filo pastry, thawed

METHOD
1 Preheat the oven to 190°C/375°F/Gas Mark 5. Spray a baking tray with cooking spray.

2 To make the filling, place the apple, raisins and brown sugar in a large bowl and toss to mix well.

3 To make the turnovers, lay one sheet of filo on your work surface and spray all over with cooking spray. Lay the second filo sheet on top and spray that one all over with cooking spray. Lay the third sheet on top. Using kitchen scissors, cut the stack lengthways into three long strips.

4 Place a heaped tablespoon of the filling at one end of one of the strips, leaving about 5 cm/2 inches at the end. Fold the uncovered end over the filling at a 45-degree angle. Continue folding end over end to form a triangular, fully enclosed bundle. Repeat with the other two strips and set the triangles on the baking tray. Repeat the entire process with the remaining three sheets of filo and the rest of the filling.

5 Spray the turnovers lightly with cooking spray. Bake in the preheated oven for about 15 minutes or until the turnovers are lightly coloured and crisp. Serve warm or at room temperature.

Vanilla Soufflé Omelettes

 calories 163 fat 8g sat fat 4.5g total sugars 8.5g carbs 12g

INGREDIENTS
serves 4

8 egg whites
2 tbsp honey,
    plus extra for drizzling
1½ tsp cornflour
2 tsp vanilla extract
225 g/8 oz ricotta cheese
sunflower oil, for brushing
200 g/7 oz raspberries

METHOD

1 Whisk the egg whites in a large, grease-free bowl until they form soft peaks.

2 Add the honey, cornflour and vanilla and whisk to mix evenly. Beat the ricotta in a small bowl until smooth, then fold lightly into the egg white mixture.

3 Brush a large heavy-based frying pan with oil and put over a medium heat. Spoon one quarter of the egg white mixture into the pan and spread evenly with a palette knife.

4 Cook for 3–4 minutes or until a golden colour underneath. Turn the omelette over and cook for 2–3 minutes on the other side, then sprinkle with one quarter of the raspberries. Gently lift one side with the palette knife and fold the omelette in half to enclose.

5 Cook for a further few seconds, then flip over on to a serving plate. Keep warm and repeat with the remaining mixture to make a total of four omelettes. Serve immediately, drizzled with honey to taste.

Lemon-glazed Gingerbread Cake

 calories 237

 fat 10.9g

 sat fat 1g

 total sugars 17g

 carbs 32.8g

INGREDIENTS

serves 16

cooking spray
150 g/5½ oz plain flour
150 g/5½ oz wholemeal flour
1 tbsp ground ginger
1½ tsp ground cinnamon
1 tsp salt
1 tsp baking powder
½ tsp bicarbonate of soda
125 ml/4 fl oz treacle
150 ml/5 fl oz hot water
100 g/3½ oz soft light brown
    sugar
100 ml/3½ fl oz rapeseed oil
85 g/3 oz unsweetened apple
    sauce
2 eggs, beaten

glaze

100 g/3½ oz icing sugar
3 tbsp lemon juice
1 tbsp finely grated lemon rind

METHOD

1 Preheat the oven to 180°C/350°F/Gas Mark 4. Spray a 25-cm/10-inch Bundt cake tin with cooking spray.

2 In a medium-size bowl, whisk together the flours, ginger, cinnamon, salt, baking powder and bicarbonate of soda. Put the treacle in a large heatproof bowl and pour the hot water over it, then mix until blended. Mix in the brown sugar, rapeseed oil, apple sauce and eggs until combined. Slowly add the flour mixture, beating until combined.

3 Transfer the mixture to the prepared Bundt tin and bake in the preheated oven for about 30 minutes or until a cocktail stick inserted into the centre comes out clean. Remove from the oven and leave to cool for about 15 minutes, then turn it out on to a wire rack and leave to cool completely.

4 To make the glaze, stir together the icing sugar, lemon juice and rind until smooth. Drizzle the glaze over the cooled cake. Slice the cake into wedges and serve at room temperature.

Salted Caramel Bread Pudding

 calories 247 fat 5g sat fat 2g total sugars 28g carbs 43g

INGREDIENTS

serves 8

cooking spray
225 g/8 oz wholemeal bread,
    cut into cubes
225 ml/8 fl oz light evaporated
    milk
175 ml/6 fl oz skimmed milk
2 eggs
85 ml/3 fl oz maple syrup
1 tsp vanilla extract
½ tsp ground cinnamon
1 cooking apple, cored and cut
    into 1-cm/½-inch cubes

sauce

15 g/½ oz unsalted butter
100 g/3½ oz soft light brown
    sugar
1 tbsp whisky
5 tbsp milk
pinch of salt
¾ tsp vanilla extract

METHOD

1 Preheat the oven to 180°C/350°F/Gas Mark 4. Spray a 20-cm/8-inch square baking dish with cooking spray.

2 Put the bread cubes on a baking tray and bake in the preheated oven for about 6–8 minutes or until they just begin to brown. Leave the oven on.

3 In a large bowl, whisk together both types of milk, the eggs, maple syrup, vanilla extract and cinnamon. Add the apple cubes and bread. Leave the mixture to stand, stirring occasionally, until the bread soaks up the liquid.

4 To make the sauce, combine the butter, brown sugar and whisky in a small saucepan over a medium–high heat and cook, swirling the pan, until the sugar has dissolved. Add the milk and the salt and bring to the boil. Boil for about a further 5 minutes until the mixture thickens. Remove from the heat and stir in the vanilla extract.

5 Transfer the bread mixture to the prepared baking dish, drizzle over the sauce and bake in the preheated oven for about 45 minutes or until it puffs up and begins to colour around the edges. Serve immediately.

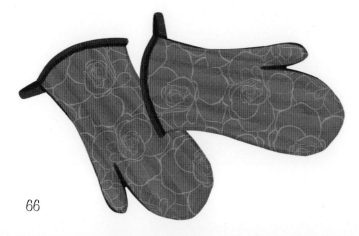

Apple & Berry Crumble

calories 237 | fat 7g | sat fat 4g | total sugars 38g | carbs 48g

INGREDIENTS
serves 8

cooking spray
6 crisp dessert apples, peeled, cored and sliced
70 g/2½ oz dried cranberries or dried cherries
4 tbsp caster sugar
½ tsp vanilla extract

topping

60 g/2¼ oz plain flour
100 g/3½ oz soft light brown sugar
½ tsp ground cinnamon
pinch of salt
55 g/2 oz butter, at room temperature
50 g/1¾ oz porridge oats

METHOD

1 Preheat the oven to 190°C/375°F/Gas Mark 5. Spray a baking dish with cooking spray.

2 To make the filling, put the apples, dried fruit, sugar and vanilla extract into a medium-size bowl and toss to mix thoroughly. Spread the mixture in the prepared baking dish, overlapping the apples a little as necessary.

3 To make the topping, combine the flour, brown sugar, cinnamon and salt in the bowl of a food processor or in a large mixing bowl. In the processor, or using two knives, cut the butter into the flour mixture until it resembles coarse breadcrumbs. Stir in the oats.

4 Sprinkle the topping evenly over the filling and bake in the preheated oven for about 45 minutes or until the topping is crisp and beginning to colour. Serve immediately.

Maple & Peach Quinoa Pudding

calories 180	fat 3.2g	sat fat 0.8g	total sugars 20.5g	carbs 31g

INGREDIENTS
serves 6

cooking spray
85 g/3 oz quinoa
500 ml/18 fl oz water
500 ml/18 fl oz skimmed milk
2 eggs
85 ml/3 fl oz maple syrup
60 g/2¼ oz unsweetened
    apple sauce
325 g/11½ oz peaches, peeled,
    stoned and diced
2 tbsp soft light brown sugar

METHOD

1 Preheat the oven to 180°C/350°F/Gas Mark 4. Spray 6 x 175 ml/6 fl oz ramekins with cooking spray.

2 In a small saucepan, combine the quinoa with the water and bring to the boil. Reduce the heat to low, cover and simmer for about 15 minutes or until the quinoa is tender. Drain well in a fine-meshed sieve.

3 In a medium-size bowl, whisk together the milk, eggs, maple syrup and apple sauce until well combined. Stir in the quinoa and divide the mixture between the prepared ramekins. Bake in the preheated oven for about 35–40 minutes or until completely set.

4 Spray a non-stick frying pan with cooking spray and heat it over a medium heat. Add the diced peaches and cook, stirring frequently, until heated through. Remove the pan from the heat and sprinkle the brown sugar over the peaches. Stir until the sugar melts and coats the peaches evenly. Set aside to cool.

5 Spoon the peaches equally over the puddings. Serve warm or at room temperature.

Pumpkin Puddings with Whipped Cinnamon Topping

 calories 232

 fat 4.4g

 sat fat 1.4g

 total sugars 30.7g

 carbs 37.6g

INGREDIENTS
serves 4
custard
900 g/2 lb pumpkin or butternut squash, halved, seeds and pulp removed, and cut into wedges
cooking spray
3 eggs, beaten
70 g/2½ oz soft light brown sugar
125 ml/4 fl oz skimmed milk
1 tbsp plain flour
2 tsp vanilla extract
¼ tsp ground cinnamon
pinch of nutmeg
pinch of salt

topping
1 egg white
2 tbsp caster sugar
¼ tsp cream of tartar
4 tbsp light evaporated milk, chilled
½ tsp vanilla extract
⅛ tsp ground cinnamon

METHOD
1 Preheat the oven to 180°C/350°F/Gas Mark 4. Put the pumpkin wedges into a roasting tin and bake in the preheated oven for 45 minutes, until soft, then scrape the flesh from the skin and purée in a food processor. Meanwhile, spray 4 x 175 ml/6 fl oz ramekins with cooking spray.

2 In a medium-size bowl, combine the eggs, pumpkin purée, sugar, milk, flour, vanilla extract, cinnamon, nutmeg and salt. Mix well. Spoon the mixture into the prepared ramekins, dividing it equally. Place the filled ramekins in a baking dish and pour boiling water into the dish so that it comes about halfway up the sides of the ramekins. Bake in the preheated oven for about 35 minutes until the puddings are set. Transfer to a wire rack to cool.

3 To make the topping, put the egg white and sugar into a bowl set over a saucepan of simmering water and whisk until the mixture is warm to the touch and the sugar is completely dissolved. Add the cream of tartar and beat with an electric whisk fitted with a whisk attachment until stiff peaks form. Add the evaporated milk, vanilla extract and cinnamon and whisk until the mixture holds soft peaks.

4 Serve the puddings in the ramekins either warm or at room temperature, topped with a spoonful of the whipped topping.

Go For It!

Are you a guilt-free girl who hates to exercise? Would you rather spend an afternoon at the dentist than go to the gym? Well, guess what? Even if you hate exercising with a fiery passion (or you are just too lazy or busy to make it to the gym on a regular basis), don't worry. You can be healthy without spending all your free time working out. Work more activity into your day, every day, and you'll be well on your way to a healthy body (and appetite)!

Getting more exercise while you go about your normal life is easy. You have to cook, clean up, do laundry and so forth anyway, so you might as well get credit for it, right? Here are how many calories the average person burns while doing everyday activities:

Grocery shopping (60 minutes): **150**

Ironing (10 minutes): **25**

Cooking (60 minutes): **85**

Washing dishes (60 minutes): **75**

Putting away groceries (10 minutes): **30**

Cleaning the house (60 minutes): **150**

Gardening (60 minutes): **240**

Even better, you can even use exercise as an excuse to have more fun such as more time spent shopping for shoes or gossiping with your girlfriends. Here's how many calories the average woman burns in 60 minutes of some of the more enjoyable activities:

Taking a leisurely walk to enjoy the spring flowers or stop and get a frothy skinny cappuccino: **200**

Shopping for the perfect pair of strappy heels or knee-high boots: **150**

Getting the latest gossip from your friends (while taking a brisk walk, of course): **300**

Shaking it on the dance floor: **400**

So if you really want to burn some calories, you could spend the day cleaning your house or working in the garden. Better yet, walk with a girlfriend to get your caffeine fix, then head to the shopping centre for a good three-hour shopping expedition (in which you could easily burn more than 650 calories!), head out to a dance club with your partner and spend an hour getting down on the dance floor.

You will have easily earned yourself any of the desserts in this book, and maybe even two servings!

Pistachio Angel Cake

 calories 170

 fat 3g

 sat fat 0.3g

 total sugars 22g

 carbs 32g

INGREDIENTS
serves 8
sunflower oil, for greasing
6 egg whites
¾ tsp cream of tartar
150 g/5½ oz caster sugar
1 tsp vanilla extract
40 g/1½ oz pistachio nuts, finely
    chopped
85 g/3 oz rice flour, plus extra
    for dusting
fresh fruit, to serve

METHOD
1 Preheat the oven to 160°C/325°F/Gas Mark 3. Grease a 1.5-litre/2½-pint cake ring tin and dust lightly with a little flour, tipping out the excess.

2 Whisk the egg whites with an electric whisk in a large, grease-free bowl until they hold soft peaks. Stir the cream of tartar into the sugar in a small bowl, then gradually whisk into the egg whites, beating at high speed until the mixture holds stiff peaks. Beat in the vanilla extract.

3 In a separate small bowl, stir the pistachios into the flour. Fold the pistachio mixture into the egg white mixture lightly and evenly, using a large metal spoon.

4 Spoon the mixture into the prepared tin and tap the tin to remove any large air bubbles. Bake in the preheated oven for 25–30 minutes or until a golden colour and firm to the touch.

5 Transfer the cake on to a wire rack and leave to cool, upside down, in the tin. When cool, run the tip of a knife around the edges of the cake to loosen, then turn out on to a plate and serve with fresh fruit.

Almond Cupcakes with Poached Pears

 calories 217

 fat 4.2g

sat fat 1.5g

total sugars 32.6g

carbs 43g

INGREDIENTS

makes 12

1.4 litres/2¼ pints water
200 g/7 oz caster sugar
6 small pears, halved, peeled and cored
1 cinnamon stick

topping

1 egg white
2 tbsp caster sugar
¼ tsp cream of tartar
4 tbsp light evaporated milk, chilled
½ tsp vanilla extract
½ tsp ground cinnamon

almond cupcakes

cooking spray
85 g/3 oz ground almonds
85 g/3 oz plain flour
½ tsp baking powder
⅛ tsp salt
25 g/1 oz unsalted butter
100 g/3½ oz caster sugar
1 tsp vanilla extract or almond extract
1 egg

METHOD

1 To make the poached pears, put the water and sugar into a large saucepan and bring to the boil. Reduce the heat to a simmer and cook, stirring, until the sugar has dissolved. Add the pears and cinnamon stick and simmer gently for about 20 minutes until the pears are tender. Drain the pears, discarding the cooking liquor, and set aside.

2 To make the topping, put the egg white and sugar in a heatproof bowl set over a saucepan of simmering water, and whisk until the sugar has completely dissolved. Add the cream of tartar and whisk with an electric whisk for about 3 minutes or until stiff peaks form. Add the evaporated milk, vanilla extract and cinnamon and whisk until the mixture holds soft peaks. Chill until ready to serve.

3 To make the almond cupcakes, preheat the oven to 180°C/350°F/Gas Mark 4. Spray a mini muffin tin with cooking spray. Combine the ground almonds, flour, baking powder and salt in a medium-size bowl. In a large bowl, cream together the butter and sugar with an electric whisk until light and fluffy. Add the vanilla extract and the egg and beat on medium–high speed until combined. Add half of the flour mixture and beat on medium–high speed until incorporated. Add the remaining flour and beat until incorporated.

4 Spoon the mixture into the prepared muffin tin, filling each hole about one third full. Bake in the preheated oven for 13–14 minutes, or until the cupcakes just begin to colour around the edges. Remove the cupcakes from the tin and serve warm with half a poached pear and a spoonful of whipped topping.

Fresh, Fruity & Fabulous!

Berry & Rhubarb Cheesecake Bars

calories 149	fat 4g	sat fat 1.5g	total sugars 16.3g	carbs 22.3g

INGREDIENTS

makes 8

cooking spray
70 g/2½ oz digestive biscuits
1 tbsp soft light brown sugar
15 g/½ oz unsalted butter, melted
1 tsp water
115 g/4 oz fresh mixed berries (blackberries, blueberries, strawberries or raspberries, diced if large)
125 g/4½ oz fresh rhubarb, diced

filling

225 g/8 oz fat-free cream cheese
55 g/2 oz honey
2 eggs, lightly beaten
1 tsp vanilla extract
1 tsp grated lemon rind

METHOD

1 Preheat the oven to 180°C/350°F/Gas Mark 4. Spray a 20-cm/8-inch square baking tin with cooking spray.

2 Pulse the digestive biscuits and brown sugar in a food processor until coarsely ground. Add the melted butter and the water and whizz until the mixture is moist. Press the mixture into the prepared tin in an even layer. Bake the base in the preheated oven for about 10–12 minutes or until it begins to colour. Remove from the oven, leaving the oven on, and leave to cool while you prepare the filling.

3 To make the filling, beat together the cream cheese and honey with an electric whisk until smooth. Add the eggs, vanilla extract and lemon rind and beat until fluffy.

4 Spread the cream cheese mixture on top of the cooled base in an even layer. Sprinkle the berries and rhubarb evenly over the top. Bake in the preheated oven for about 30 minutes or until the filling is mostly set. Remove from the oven and leave to cool to room temperature, then refrigerate to chill completely for about 2 hours.

5 Slice into 8 bars and serve chilled.

Grilled Fruit Kebabs

 calories 164 fat 8g sat fat 0.5g total sugars 22g carbs 22g

INGREDIENTS
serves 4
2 tbsp hazelnut oil
2 tbsp honey
juice and grated rind of 1 lime
2 pineapple slices,
    cut into chunks
8 strawberries
1 pear, cored and
    thickly sliced
1 banana, thickly sliced
2 kiwi fruits, quartered

METHOD
1 Preheat the grill to medium. Mix together the oil, honey and lime juice and rind in a large shallow dish. Add the fruit and turn to coat. Cover and leave to marinate for 10 minutes.

2 Thread the fruit on to four metal skewers, beginning with a pineapple piece and ending with a strawberry.

3 Brush the kebabs with the marinade and cook under the preheated grill, brushing frequently with the marinade, for 5 minutes. Turn the kebabs over, brush with the remaining marinade and grill for a further 5 minutes. Serve immediately.

Port-roasted Cherries with Vanilla Topping

 calories 137

 fat trace

 sat fat trace

 total sugars 26.2g

 carbs 28.2g

INGREDIENTS

serves 4

port-roasted cherries

300 g/10½ oz stoned, ripe fresh cherries

2 tbsp caster sugar

4 tbsp ruby port

topping

1 egg white

2 tbsp caster sugar

¼ tsp cream of tartar

4 tbsp light evaporated milk, chilled

½ tsp vanilla extract

1 vanilla pod

METHOD

1 Preheat the oven to 230°C/450°F/Gas Mark 8.

2 Put the cherries in a baking dish and sprinkle the sugar over them. Roast in the preheated oven for about 10 minutes or until the cherries soften and juice begins to leak out. Remove the dish from the oven and pour the port over the cherries, stirring to coat the cherries and deglaze the dish. Return the dish to the oven for a further 5 minutes or until the liquid begins to bubble and thicken.

3 To make the topping, put the egg white and sugar in a heatproof bowl set over a saucepan of gently simmering water and whisk until the mixture is warm to the touch and the sugar has completely dissolved. Add the cream of tartar and beat with an electric whisk until stiff peaks form. Add the evaporated milk and vanilla extract. Using a sharp knife, split the vanilla pod lengthways and scrape the seeds into the egg white mixture. Beat for a further 3 minutes or until the mixture holds soft peaks.

4 Serve the cherries warm in dessert glasses or martini glasses, topped with a spoonful of the whipped topping.

Fig & Watermelon Salad

calories 196 | fat 1g | sat fat 0.5g | total sugars 44g | carbs 43g

INGREDIENTS
serves 4
1.5 kg/3 lb 5 oz watermelon
115 g/4 oz seedless black
   grapes
4 figs

syrup dressing
1 lime
grated rind and juice of
   1 orange
1 tbsp maple syrup
2 tbsp honey

METHOD
1 Cut the watermelon into wedges and scoop out and discard the seeds. Cut the flesh away from the rind, then chop the flesh into 2.5-cm/1-inch cubes. Put the watermelon cubes in a bowl with the grapes. Cut each fig lengthways into eight wedges and add to the bowl.

2 Grate the lime and mix the rind with the orange rind and juice, maple syrup and honey in a small saucepan. Bring to the boil over a low heat. Pour the mixture over the fruit and stir. Leave to cool. Stir again, cover and chill in the refrigerator for at least 1 hour, stirring occasionally.

3 Divide the fruit salad equally between four bowls and serve.

Grilled Stone Fruit

calories 172 · fat 5.4g · sat fat 2.1g · total sugars 21.2g · carbs 27g

INGREDIENTS

serves 6

375 g/13 oz low-fat ricotta
  cheese
2 tsp freshly grated orange rind
3 firm, ripe peaches, stoned and
  quartered
3 firm, ripe nectarines,
  stoned and quartered
3 ripe plums, apricots or figs,
  stoned and halved or
  quartered
2 tbsp orange blossom honey
2 tbsp flaked almonds

METHOD

1 In a medium-size bowl, stir together the ricotta and orange rind.

2 Preheat the grill to medium–high and grill the fruit, cut side down, turning once or twice, for about 5 minutes or until they are softened and beginning to caramelize.

3 To serve, spoon the ricotta into six small dessert bowls or cups. Top each with some grilled fruit, drizzle with the honey and sprinkle the almonds over the top. Serve immediately.

What's on the guilt-free dessert menu?

Living the guilt-free lifestyle helps you to think about what you are eating and to plan ahead so you always have delicious, but healthy, snacks at your fingertips. It is a good idea to keep some sweet treats in the storecupboard as a standby. Why not make a batch of our Toffee Popcorn Bites as these small treats can satisfy hunger pangs between meals? Don't wait until you are starving before choosing your snack. That's how you end up making bad choices – trust us, we know!

Before you go grocery shopping make a list. Include healthy ingredients such as raspberries, peaches and apples on the list. Take care to list plenty of healthy, sweet snacks – yogurts, dried fruits, smoothies, frozen yogurt. If you've got a refrigerator full of fresh, healthy ingredients, you'll be more tempted to reach for a piece of fruit or yogurt when hungry.

Dice up any large fruits such as melons or pineapples so that they'll be an inviting, easy and appetizing snack. It's also easy to freeze batches of diced fruit so you can buy and prepare these snacks in advance and have them on standby!

Of course, your life wouldn't be worth living if you couldn't eat out now and then too. And rest assured, you can!

Again, planning ahead can make a big difference. Check out the restaurant's menu online before you go and decide which dessert you'll order. Steer away from anything with ice cream, double cream or pastry, and opt for lighter dishes such as sorbets or baked fruits.

And when you just want something sweet and deliciously satisfying, look no further than the pages in this book. Indulge your cravings with surprisingly light Spiced Strawberry Meringue Soufflé, Grilled Stone Fruit with ricotta, honey and almonds, or our creamy tasting, but light Orange Yogurt Panna Cotta. These recipes all taste amazing and are totally guilt free!

Spiced Strawberry Meringue Soufflé

 calories 157 fat 0.3g sat fat trace total sugars 32.6g carbs 37.5g

INGREDIENTS
serves 6
650 g/1 lb 7 oz fresh
    strawberries, diced
70 g/2½ oz caster sugar
4 tbsp water
1 tbsp cornflour
1 tsp vanilla extract
½ tsp pepper

topping
3 egg whites
100 g/3½ oz caster sugar
¼ tsp cream of tartar

METHOD
1 Preheat the oven to 200°C/400°F/Gas Mark 6. Put the strawberries, sugar and water in a saucepan and bring to a simmer over a medium heat, stirring frequently. In a small bowl, combine the cornflour with 1 tablespoon of water and stir to combine. Add the cornflour mixture to the simmering strawberry mixture and cook, stirring, for about 1 minute or until thickened. Stir in the vanilla extract and pepper and remove from the heat. Set aside to cool.

2 In a large bowl, whisk the egg whites with an electric whisk on medium–high speed until they form soft peaks. Gradually add the sugar and the cream of tartar and continue to whisk on medium–high speed until stiff, glossy peaks form. Scoop about 5 tablespoons of the strawberry mixture from the saucepan and, using a spoon or a rubber palette knife, swirl it into the meringue with just a few stirs.

3 Spoon the remaining strawberry mixture into 6 x 175 ml/6 fl oz ramekins and set the ramekins on a baking tray. Top with the meringue mixture, mounding it up and using a fingertip to swirl it into peaks.

4 Place the baking tray in the preheated oven and bake for 5–6 minutes or until the peaks begin to turn a golden colour. Serve warm.

Peach Popovers

 calories 167

 fat 3g

 sat fat 1g

 total sugars 11g

 carbs 31g

INGREDIENTS
serves 4

1 tsp sunflower oil,
   plus extra for greasing
100 g/3½ oz plain flour
1 large egg white
250 ml/9 fl oz semi-skimmed milk
1 tsp vanilla extract
3 peaches, sliced
maple syrup, to serve

METHOD

1 Preheat the oven to 200°C/400°F/Gas Mark 6. Grease 12 holes in a muffin tin.

2 Put the oil, flour, egg white, milk and vanilla extract in a large bowl. Beat thoroughly to a smooth, bubbly mixture.

3 Put the prepared muffin tin in the preheated oven for 5 minutes. Remove the tin from the oven and quickly divide the peach slices between the holes of the tin and pour the mixture evenly into each hole.

4 Bake the popovers for 15–20 minutes or until well risen, crisp and a golden colour.

5 Remove the popovers carefully from the tin with a small palette knife. Serve immediately with maple syrup.

Orange Yogurt Panna Cotta

INGREDIENTS
makes 6

3 tbsp freshly squeezed orange juice
2 tsp powdered gelatine
500 ml/18 fl oz semi-skimmed milk
350 g/12 oz low-fat natural yogurt
70 g/2½ oz honey
1 tsp vanilla extract
2 tsp grated orange rind

compote

250 g/9 oz fresh or frozen blackberries
4 tbsp water
55 g/2 oz caster sugar
2 tbsp lemon juice

METHOD

1 To make the panna cotta, pour the orange juice into a small bowl and sprinkle the gelatine over the top. Set aside until the gelatine has absorbed the liquid.

2 In a medium-size saucepan, combine the milk, yogurt, honey and vanilla extract, set the pan over a medium–high heat and bring to a simmer (do not boil), stirring to incorporate the yogurt and honey. Remove from the heat, then stir in the orange rind and the moistened gelatine mixture. Whisk until the gelatine is fully dissolved. Ladle the mixture into 6 x 175 ml/6 fl oz ramekins, dividing it equally. Leave to cool to room temperature, then cover loosely and refrigerate for at least 4 hours, or until set.

3 To make the compote, combine the blackberries, water, sugar and lemon juice in a medium-size saucepan and set over a medium–high heat. Bring to the boil, then reduce heat to medium–low and simmer until the sugar has dissolved, the liquid begins to thicken and the fruit begins to break down. Remove from heat and leave to cool to room temperature.

4 Serve the panna cotta chilled in the ramekins, with the compote spooned over the top.

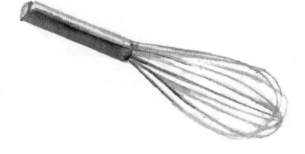

Fluffy Lemon Fools

 calories 77
 fat 0.8g
 sat fat 0.5g
 total sugars 12g
 carbs 13g

INGREDIENTS

serves 4

2 tbsp lemon juice
3 tbsp agave syrup
   or honey
1 mint sprig, plus extra
   to decorate
2 egg whites
1 tsp finely grated
   lemon rind
150 g/5½ oz low-fat Greek-style
   yogurt

METHOD

1 Put the lemon juice, syrup and mint sprig in a small saucepan over a high heat and bring to the boil, stirring. Remove from the heat and leave to stand for 10 minutes.

2 Meanwhile, put the egg whites in a large grease-free bowl and beat with an electric whisk until they hold stiff peaks.

3 Remove the mint from the syrup. Add the lemon rind to the syrup and then gradually drizzle the syrup into the egg whites, beating at high speed, until soft peaks form.

4 Add the yogurt to the egg white mixture and fold in lightly with a large metal spoon.

5 Spoon the mixture into four tall glasses or individual dishes and top each with a mint sprig. Serve immediately.

Stuffed Nectarines

 calories
93

 fat
0.2g

 sat fat
trace

 total
sugars
20g

 carbs
16g

INGREDIENTS
serves 4

4 ripe, firm nectarines
  or peaches
175 g/6 oz blueberries
125 g/4½ oz raspberries
150 ml/5 fl oz freshly squeezed
  orange juice
1–2 tsp honey, or to taste
1 tbsp brandy (optional)
4 tbsp fat-free Greek yogurt
1 tbsp finely grated
  orange rind

METHOD

1 Preheat the oven to 180°C/350°F/Gas Mark 4. Cut the nectarines in half, remove the stones, then put them in a shallow ovenproof dish.

2 Mix together the blueberries and raspberries in a bowl and use to fill the hollows left by the removal of the nectarine stones. Spoon any extra berries around the edge.

3 Mix together the orange juice, honey and brandy if using, in a small bowl and pour the liquid over the fruit. Blend the yogurt with the grated orange rind in another bowl and leave to chill in the refrigerator until required.

4 Bake the berry-filled nectarines in the preheated oven for 10 minutes or until the fruit is hot. Serve immediately with the orange-flavoured yogurt.

103

Dinner Party Showstoppers

Strawberry & White Chocolate Napoleons

calories
249

fat
8g

sat fat
2.7g

total
sugars
36g

carbs
50g

INGREDIENTS
makes 8

6 sheets frozen filo pastry,
  thawed
cooking spray
1½ tsp caster sugar
500 g/1 lb 2 oz fresh strawberries,
  sliced
2 tbsp icing sugar, to decorate

filling

100 g/3½ oz white chocolate,
  chopped
5 tbsp plus 125 ml/4 fl oz water
125 g/4½ oz caster sugar
3 egg whites
¼ tsp cream of tartar

METHOD

1 Preheat the oven to 180°C/350°F/Gas Mark 4 and cover a large baking tray with baking paper.

2 To make the filo squares, carefully separate one filo sheet from the others, lay it on your work surface, and spray it all over with the cooking spray. Sprinkle with about ¼ teaspoon of the sugar. Lay another sheet of filo over the top of the first one and repeat the steps until you have three layers. Cut the stack of filo sheets into 12 squares and transfer to the prepared baking tray. Repeat with the remaining three sheets of filo pastry so that you have 24 squares. Bake the filo squares in the preheated oven for about 6–8 minutes until lightly coloured. Remove from the oven and leave to cool completely on the tray.

3 To make the filling, put the white chocolate and the 5 tablespoons of water in a heatproof bowl set over a saucepan of gently simmering water. Heat, stirring frequently, until the chocolate has completely melted and the mixture is smooth. Set aside.

4 In a small saucepan, combine the sugar with the remaining 125 ml/4 fl oz of water and bring to the boil. Cook, stirring, for about 5 minutes or until the mixture begins to thicken.

5 Beat the egg whites in large bowl with an electric whisk until foamy. Add the cream of tartar and beat for about a further 3 minutes, gradually increasing the speed, until soft peaks form. With the mixer running, slowly add the warm sugar mixture to the egg white mixture. Increase the speed to high and beat until the mixture has cooled and stiff, glossy peaks form.

6 Whisk one third of the egg white mixture into the melted chocolate until it is well combined. Whisk in the remaining egg white mixture. Transfer the mixture to a medium-size bowl, cover and chill in the refrigerator for at least an hour.

7 Just before serving, lay eight filo squares on your work surface. Top each with about 2 tablespoons of the white chocolate mousse, then top this with four to five strawberry slices and another square of filo. Repeat with another layer of mousse and strawberries. Finish with a filo square and a dusting of icing sugar. Serve immediately.

Summer Meringue

 calories 110   fat 4g   sat fat 3g   total sugars 11g   carbs 11g

INGREDIENTS
serves 6
meringue
2 egg whites
3 tbsp caster sugar
1 tsp cornflour
1 tsp vanilla extract
1 tsp vinegar

filling
225 g/8 oz low-fat cream cheese
150 g/5½ oz low-fat plain yogurt
½–1 tsp vanilla extract,
    or to taste
300 g/10½ oz mixed berries
    (quartered or halved if large)

METHOD
1 Preheat the oven to 120°C/250°F/Gas Mark ½ and line a baking tray with baking paper. To make the meringue, whisk the egg whites in a large grease-free bowl until stiff, then gradually add the sugar, a spoonful at a time, whisking well after each addition. Stir in the cornflour, vanilla extract and vinegar.

2 When all the sugar has been added and the mixture is stiff, spoon on to the lined baking tray and form into a 15-cm/6-inch circle, hollowing out the centre to form a shell.

3 Bake in the preheated oven for 1½–2 hours or until crisp. Turn the oven off and leave to cool in the oven. Remove from the oven and leave to rest until cold before removing from the baking tray. Store in an airtight container until required.

4 To make the filling, beat together the cream cheese and yogurt in a bowl until well blended, then stir in the vanilla extract. When ready to serve, pile the cheese filling in the centre of the meringue shell, top with the fruits and serve, cut into six pieces.

Blood Orange Polenta Tart

calories 205 | fat 2.9g | sat fat 1g | total sugars 31g | carbs 40g

INGREDIENTS
serves 8

cooking spray
250 g/9 oz cooked polenta
55 g/2 oz soft light brown sugar,
    plus 1 tbsp
3 blood oranges or small
    navel oranges

filling
4 eggs
140 g/5 oz caster sugar
150 ml/5 fl oz orange juice
1 tbsp lemon juice
125 ml/4 fl oz semi-skimmed milk
½ tsp vanilla extract
1 tsp finely grated
    orange rind

METHOD

1 Preheat the oven to 180°C/350°F/Gas Mark 4. Spray a 23-cm/9-inch springform tart tin with cooking spray.

2 To make the case, combine the cooked polenta with 55 g/2 oz of the brown sugar in a medium-size bowl and mix well. Spread the mixture into a thin layer in the prepared tart tin and bake in the preheated oven for about 20 minutes or until it begins to colour.

3 To make the filling, whisk together the eggs, sugar, orange juice, lemon juice, milk and vanilla extract. Stir in the orange rind, then pour the mixture on to the polenta case in an even layer. Bake in the preheated oven for about 15 minutes or until the filling begins to set.

4 While the tart is baking, slice the oranges into thin rounds, using a serrated knife. When the filling is partly set, remove the tart from the oven and arrange the orange slices on top. Sprinkle the remaining tablespoon of brown sugar over the top and return the tart to the oven. Bake for a further 6–8 minutes, or until the filling is mostly set.

5 Remove from the oven and set the tin on a wire rack to cool. Slice the tart into wedges and serve.

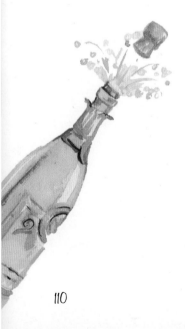

Curbing Those Cravings!

No matter how healthy your lifestyle, you're bound to battle unbeatable cravings now and then. As many a failed dieter will tell you, trying to defeat such intense urges through deprivation and sheer will is pointless. Instead, make guilt-free choices that feed your body and soul, without packing on the pounds!

Fresh fruit is always a great choice when you're craving something sweet. Juicy berries, succulent melon, crisp apples and luscious stone fruits can be surprisingly satisfying. Port-roasted Cherries with Vanilla Topping are a fantastically healthy and tasty way to add an extra serving of fruit to your day.

Sometimes a sweet sip of something warm is just the thing you need to take the edge off a sugar craving. Honey-sweetened herbal teas such as cinnamon or raspberry and hot cocoa made with skimmed milk can hit the spot on a chilly evening.

If it's a sweltering summer day and all you can think about is a cool, creamy, refreshing ice-cream cone, opt for low-fat or fat-free frozen yogurt or sorbet instead. Our Maple Ice Cream with Nut-crunch Topping, Red Wine Sorbet or Lemon Buttermilk Sorbet will do the job nicely. And you'll save yourself potentially hundreds of calories and as many as 16 grams of fat. Turn down the cone (ask for your scoop in a dish instead) and you'll save a further 25 to 100 calories.

Instead of a creamy cheesecake or chocolate pudding, try our Pumpkin Puddings with Whipped Cinnamon Topping. This is made with skimmed milk so contains all of the flavour with much less fat! Or why not try our Frozen Hot Chocolate spiked with hazelnut liqueur, made with skimmed milk and banana?

If chocolate is what you need, opt for a small serving of plain chocolate. It's lower in fat than milk chocolate, and is packed with antioxidants, healthy nutrients that reduce your risk of high blood pressure, high cholesterol and heart disease, and limit the effects of ageing on your cells. Our Chewy Chocolate Cookies deliver a double dose of rich plain chocolate because they're made with both cocoa powder and plain chocolate.

Remember the golden rule of a healthy, guilt-free girl's life: It's not deprivation, but moderation that makes keeping fit and healthy doable and, dare we say, even enjoyable.

Mini Chocolate Fondants

calories 235 | fat 10.8g | sat fat 4.2g | total sugars 19g | carbs 31g

INGREDIENTS
makes 8
cooking spray
1 tbsp plus
   1 tsp caster sugar
85 g/3 oz plain chocolate,
   chopped
20 g/¾ oz unsalted butter, cut
   into chunks
1½ tbsp milk
2½ tsp golden syrup

cake
1 egg
2 tbsp rapeseed oil
1 tsp vanilla extract
pinch of salt
50 g/1¾ oz icing sugar
40 g/1½ oz plain flour
1 tbsp cocoa powder
¼ tsp ground cinnamon
⅛ tsp ground cloves
2 egg whites
⅛ tsp cream of tartar
icing sugar, to decorate
250 g/9 oz fresh raspberries,
   to serve

METHOD

1 Preheat the oven to 180°C/350°F/Gas Mark 4. Generously coat 8 holes of a muffin tin with cooking spray. Sprinkle the teaspoon of sugar into the prepared holes, dividing it equally between them.

2 Put the chocolate and butter in a heatproof bowl set over a saucepan of gently simmering water. Heat, stirring frequently, until the chocolate has completely melted.

3 To prepare the filling, combine the remaining tablespoon of sugar and the milk in a small saucepan and bring to a simmer. Cook, stirring frequently, until the sugar is completely dissolved. Stir in the golden syrup and about one third of the melted chocolate (reserve the remainder for the cake mixture) and stir until well combined. Chill in the freezer for about 30 minutes or until firm.

4 To make the cake mixture, combine the egg, oil, vanilla extract and salt in a medium-size bowl and beat until well combined. Beat a bit of the egg mixture into the remaining chocolate until well blended. Mix the remaining egg mixture into the chocolate. Add the icing sugar, flour, cocoa powder, cinnamon and cloves and mix well.

5 In a large bowl, use an electric whisk set on medium speed to whisk the egg whites until frothy. Add the cream of tartar and continue to beat, gradually increasing the speed to high, until stiff peaks form. Gently fold the whipped egg whites into the mixture.

6 Divide half of the mixture evenly between the prepared holes of the muffin tin, placing about 1 heaped tablespoon in each. Spoon about a teaspoon of the chilled filling on top of the mixture in each hole. Spoon the remaining mixture on top, dividing it equally. Take care that the mixture is fully covering the filling.

7 Bake in the preheated oven for 8–10 minutes or until the edges begin to puff up. Remove the tin from the oven and place it on a wire rack to cool for several minutes.

8 Run a knife around the edge of each of the cakes, then place a chopping board over the top of the muffin tin and turn over the tin, releasing the cakes. Dust the cakes lightly with icing sugar and serve warm, topped with the raspberries.

Apricot & Chocolate Meringues

 calories 40
 fat 1.3g
 sat fat 0.7g
 total sugars 5.6g
 carbs 6.5g

INGREDIENTS
makes 12

6 apricots, halved and stoned
juice of ½ small orange
1 egg white
2 tbsp caster sugar
55 g/2 oz plain chocolate, cut
    into 12 pieces

METHOD

1 Preheat the oven to 180°C/350°F/Gas Mark 4.

2 Arrange the apricots, cut side up, on a baking tray. Drizzle the orange juice over the top of them. Bake in the preheated oven for 5–8 minutes.

3 Meanwhile, whisk the egg white in a large clean mixing bowl until you have stiff, moist-looking peaks. Gradually whisk in the sugar a teaspoonful at a time. Once all the sugar has been added, whisk for a further 1–2 minutes until the meringue is thick and glossy.

4 Spoon the meringue into a piping bag fitted with a medium star nozzle. Put a piece of chocolate in the centre of each apricot.

5 If the apricots wobble, stick them to the baking tray with a little meringue. Pipe a whirl of meringue on top of the chocolate. Bake in the preheated oven for 5 minutes or until the meringue is tinged a golden colour and just cooked. Leave to cool for a few minutes, then transfer to a serving plate.

Mini Key Lime Pies with Quinoa Cases

| calories 137 | fat 3.6g | sat fat 1.7g | total sugars 14g | carbs 21.8g |

INGREDIENTS
makes 20
crust
cooking spray
175 g/6 oz quinoa
55 g/2 oz cold, unsalted butter,
   cut into small pieces
½ tsp baking powder
¼ tsp salt
2 tbsp cold water
2 tbsp soft light brown sugar

filling
2 eggs
2 egg whites
125 ml/4 fl oz lime juice
finely grated zest of 1 lime
225 ml/8 fl oz light
   condensed milk
115 g/4 oz fat-free plain yogurt

topping
2 egg whites
55 g/2 oz caster sugar
¼ tsp cream of tartar

METHOD

1 Preheat the oven to 180°C/350°F/Gas Mark 4. Spray 20 holes of a 24-hole mini muffin tin with cooking spray.

2 To make the cases, put the quinoa in a food processor and whizz for about 7 minutes until it is a fine powder (there will still be some whole kernels, which is fine). Add the butter, baking powder and salt and whizz until the mixture resembles coarse breadcrumbs. Add the water and brown sugar and whizz until the mixture begins to clump.

3 Scoop about a tablespoon of the mixture into each of the holes in the prepared muffin tin. Press the mixture into an even layer in the base and all the way up the sides of each hole. Bake in the preheated oven for about 10 minutes until lightly coloured. Remove and set aside, but don't turn off the oven.

4 To make the filling, beat the eggs and egg whites in a large bowl with an electric whisk until well combined. Add the lime juice, lime zest, condensed milk and yogurt and mix well. Spoon the mixture into the baked quinoa cases, filling them almost to the top (you may end up with some leftover filling). Bake in the preheated oven for about 10 minutes or until the filling is nearly completely set. Remove from the oven and leave to cool in the tin on a wire rack. Cover loosely with clingfilm and chill for at least an hour.

5 To make the topping, preheat the oven once more to 180°C/350°F/Gas Mark 4. Put the egg whites, sugar and cream of tartar in a large bowl and beat with an electric whisk fitted with a whisk attachment on high speed until stiff peaks form. Transfer the topping to a piping bag fitted with a large, star-shaped nozzle. Pipe topping on to the centre of each mini pie in a decorative peak. Bake in the preheated oven for about 10–12 minutes or until the topping begins to colour. Transfer from the oven to a wire rack and leave to cool for about 15 minutes.

6 Run a knife blade around the edge of each pie to remove them from the baking tin. Serve warm or at room temperature.

Banana & Pecan Nut Parcels

 calories 192
 fat 5.2g
 sat fat 1.6g
 total sugars 20.6g
 carbs 31.7g

INGREDIENTS
serves 8
cooking spray
1 medium banana, mashed
30 g/1 oz pecan nut pieces
3 tbsp soft light brown sugar
16 square or round
    wonton wrappers
1 egg, beaten

sauce
15 g/½ oz unsalted butter
100 g/3½ oz soft light brown
    sugar
2 tbsp whisky
5 tbsp milk
½ tsp vanilla extract

METHOD

1 Preheat the oven to 200°C/400°F/Gas Mark 6. Line a large baking tray with baking paper and spray it with cooking spray.

2 In a medium-size bowl, combine the banana, pecan nut pieces and brown sugar and stir to mix well. Lay out the wonton wrappers on your work surface and coat the edges with the beaten egg. Put 1 tablespoon of filling in the centre of each wonton wrapper. Fold the wonton wrappers over to form semicircles or triangles and press to seal the edges. Transfer the wontons to the prepared baking tray and bake in the preheated oven for about 5 minutes or until crisp and lightly coloured. Remove from the oven and leave to cool on the tray while you make the sauce.

3 To make the sauce, combine the butter, brown sugar and whisky in a small saucepan set over a medium–high heat. Cook, swirling the pan, until the sugar has completely dissolved. Add the milk and bring to the boil. Heat for a further 5 minutes or so, until the mixture has thickened.

4 Remove from the heat and stir in the vanilla extract. Serve the wontons warm with the sauce drizzled over the top.

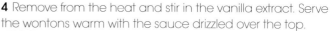